for Kevin

Each page is full of objects
from a different room in the house.

Copyright © 1992 Venice Shone
First published in Great Britain in 1992 by
ORCHARD BOOKS
96 Leonard Street, London EC2A 4RH
Orchard Books Australia
14 Mars Road, Lane Cove, NSW 2066
The right of Venice Shone as author and illustrator of this Work
has been asserted by her in accordance with the Copyright, Designs
and Patents Act, 1988.
A CIP catalogue record is available from the British Library.
1 85213 330 9
Printed in Belgium

House

VENICE SHONE

ORCHARD BOOKS

hall

bunch of keys

plant

doormat

2

broom cupboard

brush

dustpan

feather duster

shoe polish

shoe brush

mop

vacuum cleaner

broom

3

kitchen

milk pan

mixing bowl

egg whisk

frying pan

spatula

jug

grater

lemon squeezer

4

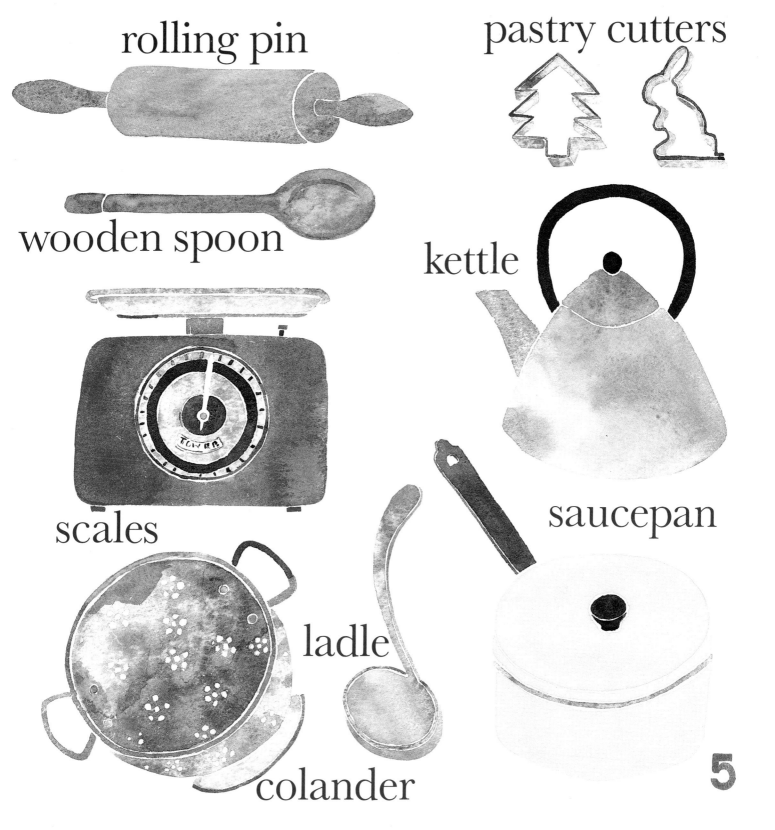

rolling pin

pastry cutters

wooden spoon

kettle

scales

saucepan

ladle

colander

5

kitchen

storage jars

6

shopping basket

tins of food

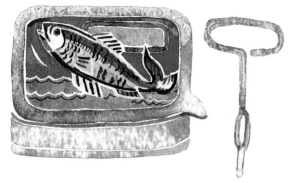

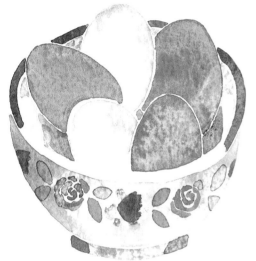

eggs

cheese

butter

7

dining room

table

tablecloth

8

high chair

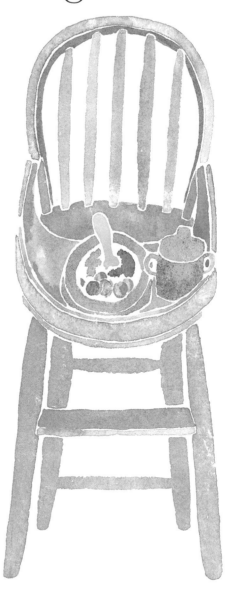

9

utility room

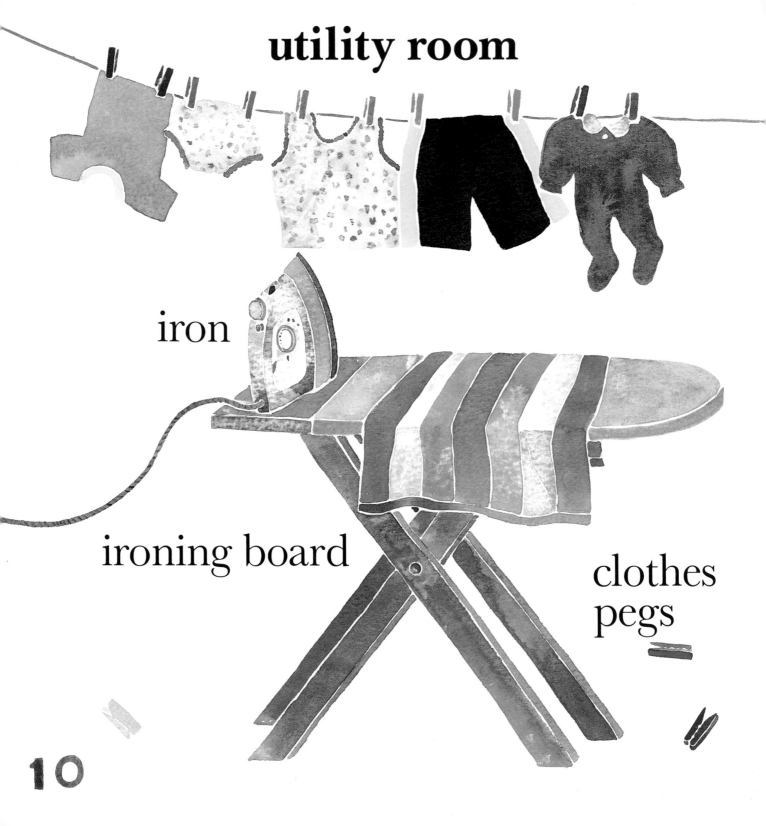

iron

ironing board

clothes pegs

10

washing line

washing

bucket

laundry basket

soap powder

11

sitting room

armchair

cup of tea

slippers

12

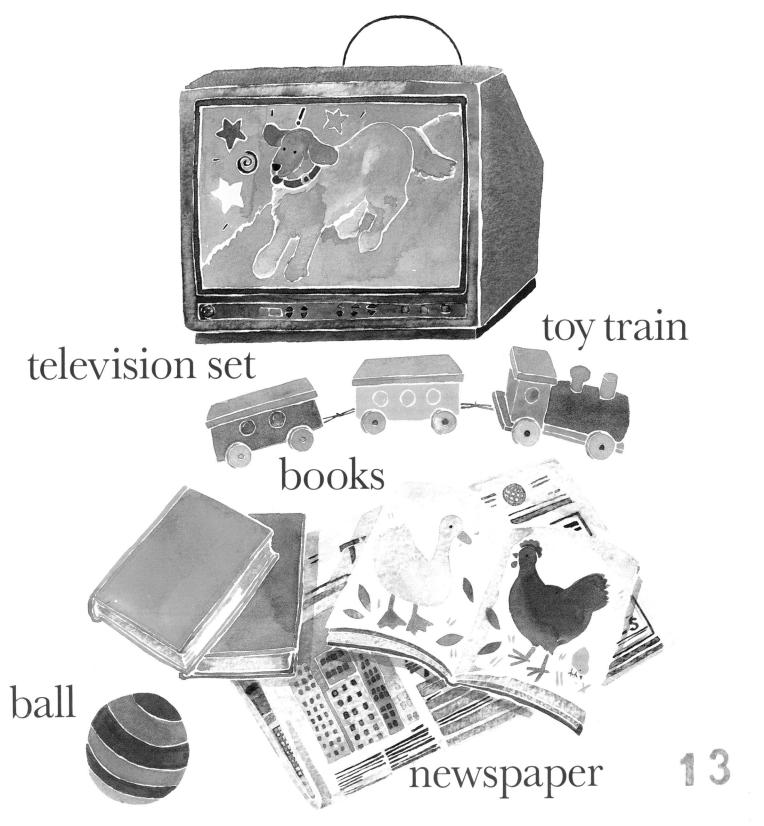

television set

toy train

books

ball

newspaper

13

study

computer

telephone

pad of
paper

INK

envelopes

rubber

pencil

pen

DIARY

0.28
calculator

14

counting
book

coloured
pencils

drawing pad

glue

paintbrush

paint box

scissors

15

playroom

yoyo

doll's house

picture books

skittles

rabbit

tricycle

16

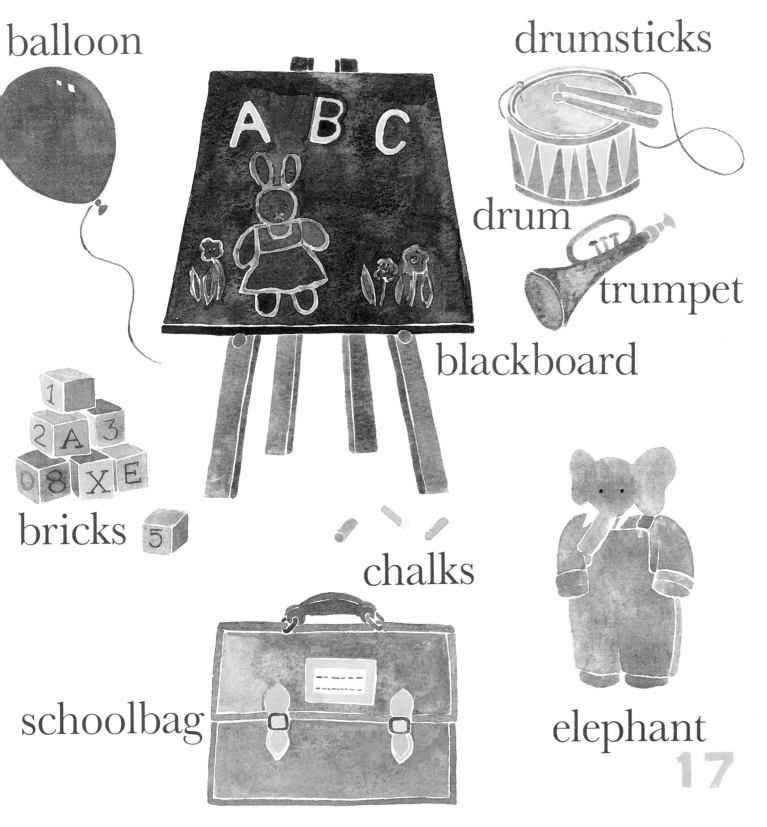

balloon

drumsticks

drum

trumpet

blackboard

bricks

chalks

schoolbag

elephant

17

bathroom

face cream

scrubbing brush

cotton sticks

BABY

soap

SHAMPOO

COLOGNE
ROSE

sponge

razor

shaving
brush

18

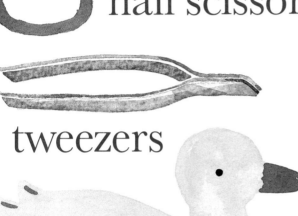

nail scissors

tweezers

flannel

rubber
duck

toothbrush

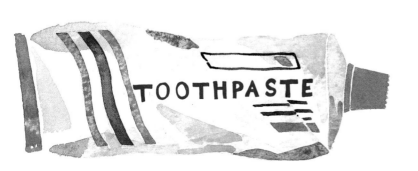

19

bedroom

pillows

quilt

20

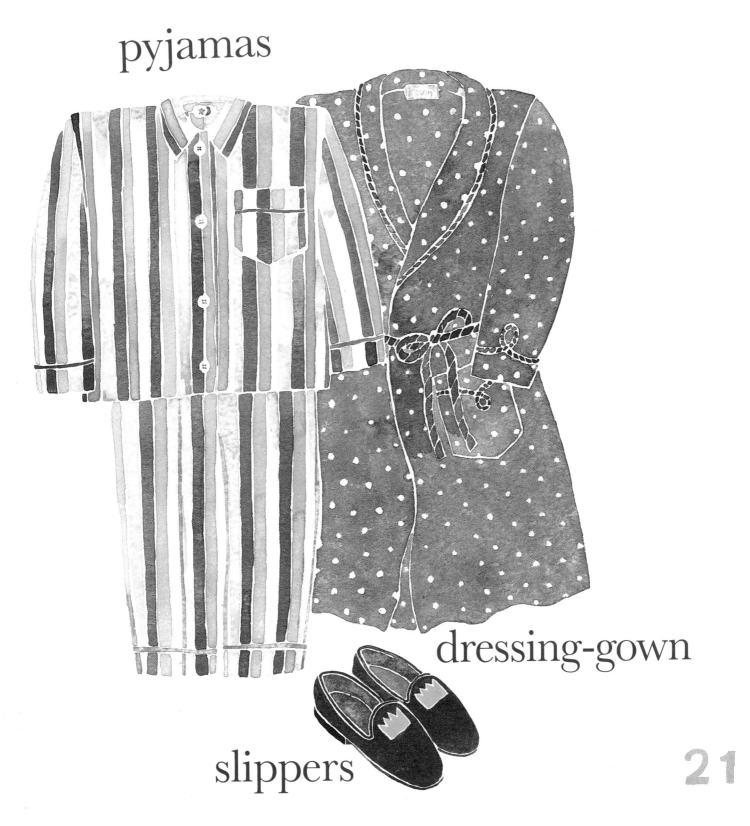

pyjamas

dressing-gown

slippers

21

bedroom

mirror

hairdryer

necklace

hair ribbon

comb

brush

perfume

lipstick

22

clock

plant

chest of drawers

23

child's bedroom

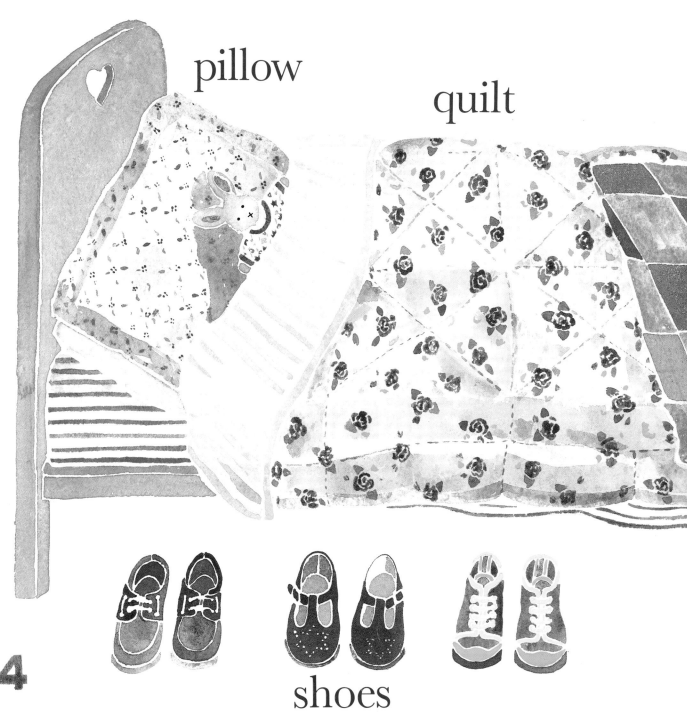

pillow

quilt

shoes

24

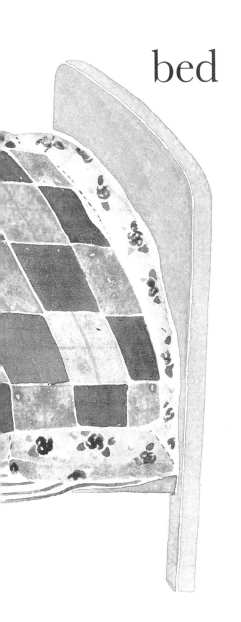

bed

pyjamas

slippers

2 5